LOVE, DEATH, AND MONEY

L♥VE,
DEA†H,
– AND –
M◆NEY

A WOMAN'S GUIDE TO LEGALLY
PROTECTING YOURSELF

NAZ BAROUTI

LIONCREST
PUBLISHING

LOVE, DEATH, AND MONEY
A Woman's Guide to Legally Protecting Yourself

ISBN   978-1-5445-1282-2 *Paperback*
       978-1-5445-1283-9 *Ebook*

This book is dedicated to any woman who has ever felt hopeless navigating through the legal system. You give me the strength to do what I do.

CONTENTS

FOREWORD

BY KERRI KASEM

I first met Naz in 2013, during a tumultuous time in my life when my family and I were in a legal battle to see my father, Casey Kasem, because my stepmother had completely blocked all access to him. She prevented my father from using his phones and computer, and she wouldn't let us in the house if we visited. The situation negatively impacted my brother, my sister, my uncle, and other family members as not a single one of us could get in to see my dad.

The legal battle made headlines, and Naz took to discussing it on her radio show where she related to the audience how cruelly my stepmother acted. Naz's producer, Debbie, reached out to me from KABC and said Naz would love to have me on the show.

I absolutely agreed.

When I first walked in and met her, I was like, "Wow. She's so young!" Having heard her on the radio, I knew Naz was extremely knowledgeable, and she sounded as if she'd been doing estate planning and law for quite a while. But I walked in, and there was this beautiful blonde, blue-eyed, gorgeous attorney, who looked like she was in her twenties. She's just very vivacious and confident, yet very warm.

I was so thankful to have met her.

From that day on, we became incredibly close and good friends. We have the same purposes in life: to help people and fight for justice. We want what's right, moral, and ethical. I love Naz and I love what she's doing. She's educating people so they don't fall into the same trap that my family fell into. She wants everyone to be prepared, especially in the subject of estate planning.

It's not a subject a lot of people like to approach. What's going to happen to you when you die? What's going to happen to your children? Who should inherit your assets? What about your animals? People don't think about these questions. They don't want to think about dying. They don't want to think about the end. But Naz is very open about it. She's like, "Kerri, we have to get this done. You can't be walking around and then something happens to you." She ran through all the possible scenarios.

This topic *must* be talked about. So many families are going through hell right now because their parents didn't create a plan for when they got sick or died. Now it's left up to the kids, and they may not know their parents' wishes, and they may not even agree with one another.

Naz's book will create awareness on a much broader spectrum. I think it's a very, very important subject.

I believe in her message so much, I asked Naz to be on my board for the Kasem Cares Foundation. She is able to give advice about probate matters, wills, and estate plans. We need that, especially when people ask us questions or for advice on any of these topics. She's there.

I also refer friends and colleagues to Naz. She works with every client one-on-one and actually sits with you. She doesn't leave it to somebody else to do. She listens to you and truly cares about you, your case, and the outcomes.

One time she told me, "Kerri, somebody came to me today, and they brought their elderly mom. They wanted to change everything in her will so it would go to them, not their siblings. It felt fraudulent." She paused for a moment and then said, "I wouldn't do it. I didn't feel the woman was competent enough. I felt like she was being manipulated." You don't see a lot of those ethics in law. Many other attorneys would have gone ahead with the changes.

There are some great attorneys out there, but most attorneys will do anything for money, like in my father's case. There's no way that someone could have said my father signed an entire power of attorney, will, and estate plan in 2011. He could understand simple things, but for an attorney to say, "Yeah, I witnessed this," that's fraudulent. That's shameful. That's criminal. There are people who will do that.

Naz is not one of them.

INTRODUCTION

The law discussed in this book is specific to California. Any legal information provided in this book is not intended as legal advice. The information provided is general in nature, and you should consult an attorney regarding your specific needs.

Mothers, wives, daughters, sisters—your opinions matter, and your assets do, too. It's imperative that you put together a will and a trust to establish your wishes, before it's too late and someone else is left to pick up the pieces.

Unfortunately, this happened to a recent client. Peter walked in my door, distraught and still in shock. His wife, Sabine, had died suddenly, leaving Peter with two young kids, a household to run, and finances to manage. He was a working physician whose wife had supported him fully and had run most everything on the domestic front, including caring for their three- and five-year-old children.

Sabine had developed pancreatic cancer, and it rapidly took her life. Shortly after she passed away, Peter came to me in need of counsel. His approach wasn't, "Where do we begin legally?" It was, "Oh my God, I just lost my wife."

Finding a lawyer is a lot like dating—you need to find someone you're comfortable with, because conversations can get very personal. Most people find me from my radio show or referrals from friends and family. Also, many big financial institutions use me as a referral. Peter was a referral, so he needed to determine if he could trust me. I did my best to put him at ease by letting him speak for a good amount of time. I don't ask questions, but just listen. He opened up and took a couple of moments to talk about his wife, her wishes, his emotions, and possible next steps.

Once he decided to move forward, Peter let me know that Sabine had inherited real property that was in her name only, but unfortunately there was no legal documentation specifying what should happen to the property in the event of her death. They hadn't planned, because they were young with young children.

Peter wanted to determine what to do with Sabine's assets:

a paid-off family home worth a million dollars and some cash in an account with her name on it. He also struggled to figure out what she would have wanted for the children. Because Sabine had no trust or will, however, the property was headed to the California courts, which would systematically distribute the assets. Without the correct documentation, the court uses California state law to distribute your assets, and you have no other option.

I told Peter that, by law, he would get one-third of the property value and his children would get the remaining two-thirds. He was shocked and dismayed, saying he didn't know if Sabine would have wanted him to have his one-third, or if the children should get it all. I had to tell him, "We don't have an option. We have to file a probate case, and the court divides per statutory guidelines."

Throughout our meeting he repeatedly said, "I wish I had had this conversation with her. I wish I had had this conversation with her." He was also concerned with the medical costs, funeral costs, and now these legal bills piling up. He didn't know where to start, and he also needed to think beyond his wife's death, to draft his own estate plan in case something happened to him. I told him that he needed to take time to grieve, but that it was also important to figure out what his wife would have wanted, so we could get the documents in order.

He needed to consider how he would care for the children and his business at the same time. He would need to have help, but would it be a babysitter, a friend, or a family member? Which caretaker would have made Sabine feel most secure? Who had more of the same beliefs?

By the end of our meeting Peter felt a little calmer, but there was a lot of pressure put on his shoulders to make these decisions without his wife's input. He left wishing that they had made these plans together as a couple, and he regretted waiting.

Many people don't want to face their mortality. It can be emotional to think about leaving children behind. Young parents feel invincible and don't want to worry about not being around to raise their children. Unfortunately, we're not bulletproof, and it's best that we put a plan in place in the event of a worst-case scenario. The first step is to find a lawyer to draft the required legal documents.

CHOOSING THE RIGHT LAWYER

There are plenty of lawyers in California who deal with estate planning, so why should you take my advice?

Estate planning (which is 90 percent of my practice) can be an emotional subject, as with Peter above. Some lawyers become robotic in this area, but I pride myself on creating a safe space for my clients during a difficult time, and I can be emotional with them, too. Recently a client came in who had just lost her father after a routine medical procedure, and he was the primary caretaker for her mother, who had Alzheimer's. After she shared her story, we cried together, and then I helped her figure out what to do to ensure that her mother was taken care of.

Even though you want an attorney to be strong for you, you also want someone who can be vulnerable and relate to your situation. You don't want cookie-cutter advice; you want someone who can step into your shoes and help you navigate what's in the best interests for you and your family. Many larger firms might have a small department that handles estate planning, but they concentrate on different areas of the law. While these attorneys may have an understanding of the subject matter, their employers put a lot of pressure on them to meet a certain number of client billable hours. They are more focused on billing the client than on taking care of the client's needs.

Whomever you choose to work with, you want them to be specialized in and have a really clear understanding of estate planning. They need to stay updated on the constant legal and tax changes. For example, I am licensed in the state of California, so the legal facts in this book are specific to California law. While the laws and regulations for estate planning are similar in many states, they can also be very, very different, and I would advise anyone outside of California to seek local legal counsel before getting started. I've been given the nickname "Estate Planning Guru" and have been called upon by such news outlets as Fox News Radio, Bloomberg TV, USA Today, and Fox 11 News for legal commentary in matters of death and divorce.

CREATING YOUR ESTATE PLAN

Licensed since 2011 as a California attorney, I am a founding partner of Barouti Law Corporation located in Southern California with offices in Brentwood, Glendale, Irvine, San Diego, and Woodland Hills. I have extensive knowledge in the areas of advanced estate planning, business planning, prenuptial/postnuptial agreements, and asset protection. I have counseled individual and corporate fiduciaries in connection with the preservation, management, and transfer of wealth, and so I tend to work with a lot of high-net-worth clients: celebrities, professionals, doctors, lawyers, business owners, and their families. I also often work with women who were successful before their marriage, or who started to make a lot of money during marriage, and now want to protect their assets.

I always say that estate planning—when you don't prepare the necessary documents—is like being in a car without your seatbelt, getting into a car accident, getting thrown out of the windshield, and sustaining a severe injury. The ambulance arrives, and you tell the paramedics, "Wait a minute, I want to go back and put my seatbelt on." When a traumatic life incident happens, you can't say you want to go back and put together those estate planning documents.

Many people don't understand what proper estate planning entails. There's a common misconception that if something happens to you, the courts don't get involved. People believe their surviving spouse can freely access their bank accounts or sell properties not jointly owned. As much as we would like things to be easy, the courts are specific about how all assets will be divided if the deceased person didn't have a plan in order.

WHAT TO EXPECT

There is a lot to cover on the topic of estate planning. This book will explain the following:

- Dictating medical decisions (including what happens if you become incapacitated)
- Making decisions around finances
- Creating wills and trusts
- Distributing your personal items, possessions, real estate, and bank accounts

- Determining your children's guardian(s)

You'll also find information on the qualities and qualifications you should look for in an attorney, how much they should charge, and what kind of documents they need to provide you.

Another important aspect to estate planning is informing your family members about your decisions. Oftentimes clients create an estate plan but don't tell the heirs or the family members they may have chosen to leave out as beneficiaries. If you don't share that information, it can cause problems in the long run when family members begin to contest the validity of the documents or argue with one another over the distributions. I'll offer some advice on this topic, and I'll also share some of my client's stories (all names have been changed to protect their privacy), so you can learn from their mistakes and avoid them yourself if you're in a similar situation. While this book is intended for women, men can apply the scenarios to their lives as well.

PART 1

—

GET THE SCOOP

It's time to set the wheels in motion and get ready to put together your estate plan. But wait. What is an estate plan, do you need an attorney, and how do you find one who has your best interests in mind? I've got all those details and more in these next few chapters.

CHAPTER 1

♥ † 💎

WHY YOU NEED A PLAN: BECAUSE THE GOVERNMENT ALREADY HAS ONE FOR YOU

And you may not like it.

If you don't have legal documents that specify what should happen after you die, the government has a plan for you. If you die without a will or trust, it's called dying "intestate" and your estate will go through probate. Probate is the legal process in which the court sees that your debts are paid and your assets are distributed according to your will. If you don't have a valid will or trust, your assets are distributed according to state law. Often the court will appoint an executor—a complete stranger who knows nothing about you or your family—who will quickly try to liquidate any assets so they can pay off all debts, take a fee for their services, and be done. Many are reading this and thinking, "What's the big deal?" Well, the probate process is expensive, takes a long time, doesn't allow for privacy, and your family has no control. Legal fees, executor fees, and other costs must be paid before your assets can be distributed to your heirs. Typically, the process can take anywhere from nine months to two years. I've seen, however, some matters that have taken over five years. In addition, probate is a public process, so any person can see what you owned. The process allows for various individuals to contest the distribution and claim they were owed a share.

Let's take the following case as an example:

A gentleman died, leaving behind assets and an estate worth over $15 million that had not been placed in a trust. His wife had passed away before him, and they had three children who stood to inherit the estate.

The government was the big winner in this case, as it took a huge chunk of the estate in taxes and probate court fees. The entire situation could have been avoided with proper estate planning. The father could have used the allotted lifetime exemption for gifting without having to pay taxes, and given the money to his children by taking advantage of the Federal Estate and Gift Tax Law. It allows an individual to transfer an unrestricted amount of assets to his or her spouse at any time, including at the death of the transferor, free from tax. Without this exception, the children were forced to sell the property just to pay the IRS.

But it got worse.

Unbeknownst to the children, their father had a child out of wedlock whom they—and he—knew nothing about. The child's mother was underage at the time when she got pregnant and chose not to put the man's name on her daughter Jane's birth certificate. As an adult, Jane learned about her father when her half sister found her. She learned about his passing, and also that she could inherit from his estate.

Jane filed a claim with the probate court because her father did not have a will. Turns out, there were several children the deceased man didn't know about, and they all came forward as heirs for a piece of the estate.

Jane certainly had to prove her case, using DNA evidence to change her birth certificate and prove to the probate court that she was a living heir, which she did.

The court divided the assets among all the children, not

just the ones the father had known about. They divided not only his assets, but also the ones he previously inherited from his wife. She had died without an estate plan, and he inherited her half of all joint assets of all their community property. Now their children had to share the combined assets of both parents equally with Jane and the other half siblings who came forward.

In order to avoid all of this, what should have Jane's father done? Even though they were married and held all assets jointly, he and his wife should have written a married revocable trust. Many believe that joint ownership avoids probate; however, it just postpones it. What would have happened if both of them were involved in a car accident and died? Don't let joint ownership deter you from writing these important legal documents. Also, another key thing to remember is that with some assets, such as real estate, all owners must sign to sell or refinance. If one of the co-owners becomes incapacitated and there is no power of attorney giving you signatory authority, the court will get involved to name an agent to sign on your behalf (I will discuss this further in another chapter).

As soon as his wife died, he should have transferred his 100 percent ownership of all assets into a trust, so if he died, it wouldn't go through probate. Within the trust he should have documented, "I don't recognize any other children." While Jane was happy she got a portion of the estate, the three children certainly were not.

When there is no will or trust, the courts decide how to divide the estate based on a specific formula, regardless of the heirs' feelings or family wishes. They don't care if heirs have a relationship with the family or not, and half relatives count as full relatives.

WHO IS ENTITLED TO WHAT?

The following table details the flow for how an estate in California is divided if there is no will or trust.

IF SOMEONE DIES WITH...

A spouse, but no children, parents, or siblings	Spouse inherits everything.
Children, but no spouse	Children inherit everything.
Parents, but no children, spouse, or siblings	Parents inherit everything.
Spouse and children	Spouse inherits all community property (property acquired during the marriage—excluding gifts or inheritances) and one-third of separate property (property owned by the deceased spouse). Children inherit two-thirds of separate property.
Spouse and parents, no siblings	Spouse inherits all community property, and half of separate property. Parents inherit half of separate property.
Spouse and siblings, no parents	Spouse inherits all community property, and half of separate property. Siblings inherit half of separate property.

TAKING CARE WITH SEPARATE PROPERTY

People are often shocked to learn how strict intestate laws are. They feel if they've been married to someone for thirty years, they should get to make the decisions about their assets, whether it's community or separate property. Unfortunately, without a will or trust, that is not the case.

It's important, especially when you're getting married, to know if your significant other is coming in with a lot of assets in just their name. This is considered separate property, and you are not entitled to all of it when your spouse dies, unless they specifically note you as the beneficiary in their estate plan. The court can only base their distribution decisions off of title and ownership of those assets.

Many of the cases I see going through probate are situations where a married couple purchased a home, but the title was only in one name, mainly because one spouse didn't qualify for a loan due to bad credit. If the couple didn't create a trust, and the spouse whose name was on the property dies, the property has to go through probate court and unexpected things can happen. An estranged child, like Jane, can come in and say she's entitled to two-thirds of the property, even though the living spouse has resided in the home and helped pay the mortgage for a decade. Or the in-laws can go to court and claim their half of the separate property.

Unfortunately, in most of these instances, the surviving spouse can't afford to continue making payments on the property, and it has to be sold to pay legal bills, taxes, and so on.

THE DIFFERENCE BETWEEN WILLS AND TRUSTS

There is a significant difference between wills and trusts, and you should know the difference. A will may not be the best decision for you and your family because a will does not avoid probate when you die. A will must be validated by the probate court before it can be enforced. In addition, a will goes into effect after you die, which means it provides no protection if you become incapacitated. This, in turn, allows the court to take control of your assets before you die. The solution in avoiding this scenario is having an attorney draft a trust. It avoids probate and lets you keep control of your assets while you are alive, incapacitated, and even after you die. I think of a trust as a piggy bank. You take all the assets you own and put them in the piggy bank, and you are the manager of that piggy bank while you're alive. You can take money out, spend it, even give it away. You can sell the assets in the piggy bank. Then, when you die, someone else steps in and manages that piggy bank and distributes the contents according to your instructions.

I should note here that even if you have a trust, you

will need a "pour-over" will that collects all assets you forgot to transfer into your trust and pours it over to your trust. Also, the will names a guardian or guardians for minor children.

There are two types of trusts—revocable and irrevocable—and it's important to know the difference before choosing the one that best fits your situation.

REVOCABLE TRUST

A revocable trust is the most common type of trust and is one that you (the grantor) can change at any time. It's the type of trust that most people establish, because they want to have flexibility and control over the assets as changes occur. You may buy or sell new items, businesses, and/or properties that you want to add to the trust. You may find that your relationships change—with your spouse, your children, or your family members—and you want to have the ability to update your trust and make the proper edits as needed.

IRREVOCABLE TRUST

An irrevocable trust is the opposite of revocable—it's not meant to be changed, except in special circumstances, and then only by the trustee and/or beneficiary. You do not manage it; you select someone else to manage it.

We often see clients using an irrevocable trust for asset protection, a way to secure their assets in case they get sued. As long as the assets are placed in the trust, they are protected. They can continue to provide for beneficiaries beyond the reach of any creditors; however, these trusts are not right for everyone. There are tax disadvantages, and these trusts can limit the client's control and use of the assets transferred.

People who use irrevocable trusts are usually those with a high net worth, or older people attempting to secure their assets because they don't want anyone—children, family members, business partners, and so on—to force them to change the trust. Let's say they've paid off real estate and want to transfer it into an irrevocable trust. They put it in and it's done! They don't have to worry about lawsuits, because creditors cannot access an irrevocable trust. However, it is important to note that irrevocable trusts should be set up before a lawsuit or potential lawsuit. The timing of the distribution of an asset into an irrevocable trust is key. The court will often consider the transfer of an asset into an irrevocable trust fraudulent when there is a pending lawsuit.

CERTIFICATE OF TRUST

The certificate of trust is a key component in using either kind of trust. It is a document created that contains crucial information about the trust without divulging personal details. The certification of trust—or trust certificate—contains primarily the trust's name, date of creation, grantor(s) identification, current trustees, trust taxpayer ID number, and the trustee's powers. If after setting up the trust you purchase a new home or obtain a new bank account, you can use the certificate to transfer title and ownership into the trust—opening the piggy bank and adding more assets to it.

ESTATE PLANNING FOR WHEN YOU'RE ALIVE

Many people think estate planning is only set up to be utilized when they're dead and gone. That's not the case; there should be two other essential documents in the estate plan or package that an attorney creates for you that can assist you while you're alive.

DURABLE POWER OF ATTORNEY

The durable power of attorney defines who steps into your shoes financially when you become incapacitated. This document determines who is able to sign your checks, talk to the IRS, and work on your behalf with financial institutions. There are two different types of durable power of attorney: one that gets triggered when you're incapacitated, called a springing power of attorney, and one for when you want someone to be able to sign for you at any time. The springing power of attorney role is important, even if you're married. Your joint assets can't be controlled if you're incapacitated. If your spouse needs to sell assets or sign documents, they wouldn't be able to do so for you without this power of attorney.

This second type is typically used by people who travel a lot for work and need someone to make financial decisions for them regularly. They're not in one place at one time and want someone to be able to buy and sell real estate, or sign checks, for them. They can give power of attorney to someone immediately and don't have to be incapacitated for that person to sign on their behalf.

ADVANCE HEALTHCARE DIRECTIVE

The advance healthcare directive, also known as a living will, allows you to define healthcare decisions in advance of a situation where you might be incapacitated. Your healthcare directive can cover any of a variety of medical topics specific to your views and religious beliefs. For example, some people's beliefs prohibit blood transfusions or require confirming with a religious official before removing you from life support. With an advance healthcare directive, even if you were unconscious, the hospital will know not to give you a transfusion. Some people don't believe in organ donation, or there are religious elements to be considered for their medical decisions, choice of doctor, or burial arrangements. Those can all be documented in the advance healthcare directive.

Another part of the advance healthcare directive is the HIPAA authorization, which allows doctors and hospitals to release medical information to the person whom you've selected to be your decision maker if you're incapacitated. It's important to name this person when someone has a rare condition or an illness, as they will need access to medical files to make health decisions. Unfortunately, even a parent or close relative can't get access without HIPAA authorization, as per federal law.

In my opinion, the advance healthcare directive is probably one of the most important parts in the estate planning process, because people are often more opinionated about what happens to their bodies versus their "stuff." It's important for all those involved, as in the case of Kerri Kasem; her stepmother was the agent for her father's healthcare directive and kept the children from seeing their father in the hospital.

DO I REALLY NEED A LAWYER?

Yes! You need a lawyer when setting up your estate plan. This is not the time to be stingy. Many avoid getting these documents because of the cost, but the unexpected can happen (like we saw with Jane's story). It's imperative that you set aside money to get your estate planning done the correct way. Don't use online services, because you may download the incorrect paperwork, fill it out incorrectly, or otherwise miss important steps in the process. An attorney who prepares the documents makes sure they are done correctly and makes sure they are validly executed and can hold up if contested.

In the next few chapters, I will show you how to get a qualified lawyer, start things off on the right foot, and learn what you should expect to pay so that there are no surprises. When an attorney prepares the documents, they ensure that everything is done correctly, is validly executed, and will hold up in court if contested.

CHAPTER 2

♥ † 💎

WHY YOU NEED A LAWYER: BECAUSE YOU GET WHAT YOU PAY FOR

There are several reasons people avoid estate planning. It's daunting to find the right lawyer, it can be expensive, and it's scary talking about your own mortality. Before you start your journey, you should know what to expect in terms of choosing a lawyer and what you will pay. Oftentimes people need to plan to set aside the necessary money needed for the process.

Many clients have come to me thinking that they already have an estate plan because they used an online resource to generate documents. Unfortunately, online services have holes in the process that most people aren't aware of. These clients selected a free preview to avoid necessary fees to get the job done right, and their documents were incomplete. I've seen documents that are not notarized, with no witnesses on the will. After their passing, if someone presented these documents in court or took them to any financial institution, the court or bank would just laugh. The documents would never hold up.

Online services aren't the only problem; there are even some offices that offer "screaming deals" on estate planning that catch people's eyes. You can drive down any major boulevard and see small offices advertise with one-liners about planning your estate for ninety-nine dollars. Clients bring in the results of the ninety-nine dollars they spent, wanting a second opinion to see if their documents look right or hoping for reassurance that they filled out the paperwork correctly. Unfortunately, they are almost never complete.

These offices essentially use a template and employ people with no legal background. The employees never take the time to walk people through the essential parts of their plan. What these offices and online services fail at is offering personalization for your needs. Every estate plan is different based on the person and his or her family. For example, if you own real estate, once the trust is created, you need to change the title of your real estate to the trust name. This is called funding the trust. For example, if I own real estate and the title of the deed is "Naz Barouti, a single woman," I would have to transfer that ownership to "Naz Barouti, trustee of the Barouti Trust." This will ensure that the real estate is owned by my trust to avoid probate after my passing. You also need a durable power of attorney and an advance healthcare directive, too. These documents are consistently overlooked.

When considering your options, is it possible to describe how you want everything in your life distributed in a template box allowing three hundred characters or less? When you forgo an attorney, you're restricting the most important elements of your life to a tiny box on a form. This is not advisable. You should interact with an attorney who knows what questions to ask, and who knows the ins and outs of estate planning. This process is not black and white, and you need someone who knows how to navigate those gray areas.

Are you scared now?

Good! Let's help you find the best partner for your plan.

FINDING YOUR BEST MATCH

When you're looking for the right lawyer for estate planning, you need to ask around, not shop around. Don't search Google and call each office you find, only to ask about their rates. Don't treat estate planning like buying tires—calling one shop and listening to them price-match or beat the shop down the street by fifty dollars. You're not buying an item; you're paying for a lawyer's time, experience, and quality of work.

It's best to start by asking for referrals or reading reviews. Talk to the attorneys you're considering. Most offer a pre-consultation appointment that allows you to meet with the attorney and discuss their experience, methods, and expenses before hiring them. At my office, we have a $200 consultation fee that gives you an hour of my time; when or if you come back, we give you a $200 credit for that. We value our time, and we believe that our clients should, too. Some attorneys don't charge a consultation fee, but in my experience they charge more for their sessions or to put together the documents. Also, be cautious of anyone who charges more than $500 for the consultation.

It's important for people to understand that the product we provide is not always tangible. When you go to a dentist's office to have a cavity filled, you feel confident paying for the dentist's services because you leave with a filling. When you go to a lawyer's office, you sometimes only leave with information—but it's valuable information that you didn't have before. Sometimes people feel that because they're paying for time and not a tangible product, their money is wasted or they shouldn't have to pay in the first place. Remember that there is a lot of value to the intangible, too.

LOOK FOR THE RED FLAGS

Always go with your gut feeling when selecting an attorney. Look for any red flags. How quickly do they respond to you, and how quickly are they able to see you? Are they going to draft your paperwork themselves, or are they going to pass it off to their paralegal? It's important to work with an attorney who will be active on your case and involved with drafting your documents.

Imagine that you sat down with an architect to build your dream house. You spent an hour or two together discussing all the details, and you wanted that architect to draw the blueprint and work on your house. If they handed the project off to someone else, or gave their notes to someone who wasn't in the meeting, the end result would not be the dream house you discussed and envisioned. Go with your women's intuition in this process. Be aware of your feelings as you select the lawyer you're going to work with.

One red flag to consider is an attorney who seems judgmental. We no longer live in a traditional bubble of what a family should look like. As society changes, so should the people whom we hire to work for us. They should be open minded; unfortunately, some attorneys are passive aggressive and judgmental about a woman being in financial control of their family, because they're not used to that scenario. Older men—and women—who are used to a conservative set of expectations often don't vibe well with a powerful female client who makes a lot of money. Their biases can work against you.

Some attorneys will not work with gay couples, for example. This is why asking around is so important.

CONSIDER YOUR SOCIAL MEDIA ASSETS

Some attorneys, especially older ones, are not always updated on managing social media accounts and how to protect online assets and image rights. If you have an online presence, you must work with someone on how to handle your online images and social media accounts. Many of my clients are celebrities and social media influencers, and their number-one concern is how to protect their image and social media rights. Since the right is a property, it can be passed on to your heirs after death. If others use their image for commercial gain, your estate can seek damages. The Celebrities Rights Act, passed in California in 1985, extended these rights to seventy years after a celebrity's death. Also important are one's digital assets. With the growth of social media, having accounts on You-Tube, Twitter, Facebook, and Instagram can generate followers and income. It is critical that your digital assets are accounted for so that your trustee is able to exercise control over your online presence and take any action they feel is appropriate. These assets have become so important that even Facebook has provided its users with the option to designate who can take over their account after death.

Believe it or not, loved ones often cannot access email or manage social media accounts once a family member has passed. I saw a family of a deceased veteran fight Yahoo! in court over access to his email account. Yahoo! maintained that, based on their guidelines, they could not release that private information. Eventually, the court ordered Yahoo! to release the emails, but it was an unexpected and time-consuming fiasco for the family.

Facebook actually has a setting that allows users to determine who will handle their profile if something happens to them. You can also select a moderator for your page, so that in your passing, friends can memorialize you by posting pictures and memories, but your moderator can delete items that shouldn't be there. Nothing is worse than the free-for-all posts on the page of someone who is deceased. With a moderator assigned, those unfortunate outcomes can be avoided.

Some families choose to delete their deceased loved one's profile because they don't want to be reminded of their loss, and I respect that. Others are embarrassed of their loved one's social media presence. But instead of leaving the decision up to these family members, why don't you choose how you want your content handled?

Those with prominent social media accounts need to decide what happens to that asset upon their death. People are becoming celebrities via YouTube and Instagram. Your followers allow you to become an influencer, and companies and advertisers provide a passive income for promoting their products. You're golden if you have a blue check on Instagram, because it confirms you are the authentic influence or celebrity on the account. Once you have it, or any other social media clout, you want to protect it. Your lawyer needs to move along at the same speed as the technological advances in society, offering advice on what to do with those accounts should anything happen to you.

There are companies, too, that save all your usernames and passwords for a monthly fee. They hold this information securely for you, and you provide the names of those who can access your accounts if the need arises.

Technology has changed us. We do almost everything online now. When is the last time you received a bank statement in the mail? Someone needs to know all of your usernames, logins, and passwords so those accounts can be managed and maintained. Bank accounts are a given, but even subscriptions like Netflix, Hulu, and Dropbox are expenses that require management. It's particularly easy for online subscriptions to be overlooked, and years down the road after someone dies, people discover they've been paying thousands of dollars unnecessarily and wastefully. Attorneys who are not up to date with legal changes in the technology world will fail you with estate planning, because these elements are all important.

I personally welcome all clients, from all aspects of life, and I'm definitely up to speed on technology advancements and assets to help those clients. Youth has its advantages. I ask my clients, "Don't you want an attorney who is going to outlive you when it comes to this stuff?" Trust me, you don't want an attorney who is going to die before you. They help you plan, then they're gone.

ASSESS A LAWYER'S REPUTATION

Once you're considering a specific attorney, make sure to research them on your state bar's website. Enter their name to see if they have any public cases where they violated the law and if they are either suspended or disbarred. Believe it or not, there are attorneys who have been suspended several times and are still not disbarred.

I work with clients who have used suspended attorneys—the clients pay money, sign a retainer agreement, and then find themselves in trouble down the road. My first question when they come to me for help is, "Did you check them online with the California State Bar to verify that there were no claims against them?"

All claims against attorneys are listed on the website. If attorneys have been unethical or in violation of the law, you'll see it there, in all its detailed glory. This tool is vital to verify your choice.

Google reviews are also a good tool. Use them cautiously, however, because we've all seen negative, inaccurate Yelp and Google reviews from people who are just angry. Ask around and talk to people who have used the attorney you're considering to see what their experience was like.

REVIEW THE RETAINER AGREEMENT

Once you find an attorney, make sure to review the retainer agreement. This agreement serves to govern the terms of your attorney/client relationship and should include scope and goals of engagement, estimation of fees, and how any disputes will be handled. If you're married, you can sign a conflict waiver and choose to have the attorney represent the both of you together. Another option is to seek separate legal counsel.

Often, women attend meetings arranged by their husbands or partners with an attorney whom the significant other has selected. In this scenario, women think that the attorney is there to protect them, and they're not— they're there to protect their spouse. There are a lot of shady attorneys who don't obtain a conflict of interest waiver, and without a signed conflict of interest waiver, they're only representing the spouse. Even worse, these attorneys will rarely make it clear who they are representing, so the wife signs documents with elements that are not in her best interest.

It's possible that an attorney will state that they are not representing you, and that you're not covered on the retainer. This is when you get your own attorney to review the documents.

THE EXPECTED PAYMENT RANGE

When it comes to estate planning, depending on the complexity of your assets, you can expect to pay the lawyer you've selected anywhere from $1,000 to $10,000. Rarely should the number fall outside this range, so if you are quoted a higher amount, be cautious. Once, I had a bank representative come into my office and request a quote for a customer. They were surprised with the quote I provided—not because it was high, but because a huge Los Angeles law firm quoted $100,000, when the job could be done within $5,000. This big firm knew that the potential client was very wealthy, so they inflated their price.

Regardless of your situation, make sure that the lawyer is not charging fees based on your wealth or their judgments of your wealth because of how you dress or present yourself.

If you're single, you can expect to pay, on average, anywhere from $1,000 to $2,500. If you're married, anywhere from $2,500 to $5,000 is normal. The number of bank accounts you have doesn't impact these estimates, but your real estate does. For every property you own, a recording fee must be processed to transfer title ownership from your individual name to the name of the trust. This recording fee is assigned, as well as a fee for the document preparation. The fee also covers county filing fees and messenger fees. This process must be completed for each property, resulting in an increase of anywhere from $200 to $400 per property. However, there are some attorneys who add this fee in the original quote for the preparation of estate planning documents.

Depending on the size of your estate and assets, there might be a need to do additional estate planning, or a need for different forms of estate and tax planning. More than one document may need to be drafted, in addition to the documents I've already mentioned. If your estate is over the federal exemption amounts, I would consult with a tax advisor to ensure that you are using all resources to pass on the estate without paying a lot of taxes. This can all result in additional fees.

The initial consult fee discussed earlier should be credited to the first invoice. Consult fees are typically between $100 and $500. If your attorney is charging you more than $500, you probably want to rethink working with them.

POSSIBLE ATTORNEYS TO AVOID

If you have a family member who is a lawyer, they can help you with your estate planning as long as they are not an interested party. However, I would advise not working with them as it can create various conflicts of interest. If you are set on using a family member, I would recommend having a second attorney independently review your documents.

For instance, you may ask your cousin to draft your trust. He's not mentioned anywhere as a beneficiary or a trustee, but because he drafted it, it is highly recommended that you pay another attorney for an independent review. They will review the document to make sure your cousin did not include items in his personal interest, ask if the document is what you want, and ask if you were coerced into it. If the document is accurate and you were not coerced, they sign off on it. Using family members is not advisable, and the extra step of an independent review is a little tedious.

Some people consider lawyers from other practice areas for estate planning. The legal profession is very specific to a lawyer's area of expertise, and you shouldn't go to someone for estate planning just because they're a lawyer. Just as you wouldn't go to an ob-gyn if you had heart problems, you wouldn't go to a patent attorney for estate planning. Make sure estate planning is their specialty; after all, this is a long-term relationship. You'll see this lawyer many times, and as your life changes, you'll go back to them to change your documents. You want your attorney to be specialized, available, accessible, and alive. As I said before, your estate planner should be able to move along with you throughout your journey. You want them to know any changes or additions to laws, because that—and that alone—is what they practice.

Once you've chosen your attorney and drafted your estate plan, it's time to talk to all the beneficiaries and family members involved, and perhaps those who aren't.

♥ † 💎

CHAPTER 3

WHY YOU NEED GUTS AND TISSUES: BECAUSE IT'S IMPORTANT TO TALK TO EVERYONE AFFECTED BY YOUR ESTATE PLAN

The estate planning process is an extremely important one, and it requires critical discussions—both when putting the plan together and after it's in place. Family members need to know the reasoning behind your choices so they aren't upset later—or try to battle it out with the other beneficiaries.

It becomes a tricky situation, for instance, when couples come into my office without discussing beforehand who they want to name as guardians of their minor children. I've seen huge arguments erupt when they think their spouse agrees with their selection, only to find out the opposite.

When this happens, I tell the couple to each make a list of the top five people whom they trust to raise their children and run the children's finances. Then they look at where the lists overlap. In an ideal situation, this would be done by a couple prior to our meeting, not taking up billable time in my office.

These preliminary conversations give you the time and space to come up with questions you didn't know you had, or to discuss topics that you didn't think about initially. The result is a plan that relieves your partner—and others who love you—of a huge burden in a time of crisis. They won't have to attempt to piece together your wishes, and they will know why you chose specific people to make decisions for you—whether they be financial or medical.

THE IMPORTANCE OF BEING PROACTIVE

I have had clients who failed to discuss their decisions with family members, and the results were rarely pleasant. One couple neglected to discuss their plan with the wife's sister. She came over one day, saw the legal binder on the kitchen table, and began poking around to see who they planned for guardianship of the children. She found that they had chosen a college friend instead of her to take care of the kids, as well as their finances. This discovery caused instant turmoil. The sisters had a huge falling out and didn't speak to one another for years. On top of that, the wife worried that her sister would cause problems and try to take their friend to court over the decision.

It's not fun to be blindsided, so I understand how the sister felt. She assumed that since she was family, she would take care of any important decisions in her sister's life in the event that she was unable to. But the reality is, humans have changed, and friends can become closer than siblings.

The law, however, has not changed. The law typically considers family members over anyone else to take control of your decision making and assets. This is why it's important that you discuss your estate plan with your family—especially in the instance that you select close friends unrelated to you as beneficiaries or to make decisions for you. You don't want to blindside your family, and you should take the time to explain to them—in a sensitive way—why you made your decisions. Perhaps you don't want to burden them, or maybe you want to keep your children in their current city or state. Lay out, as simply as possible, the reasons for your decisions.

WHEN TO HAVE THE DIFFICULT TALK

I find that the best time for these discussions is over the holidays. This may seem counterintuitive, since tensions can run high, family members may not have seen each other in a while, and alcohol is often involved. However, it's during the holidays that we all come together and remember why we love our family—and why we don't. It's so hard to find a random day that works for everyone during the rest of the year. When they are already gathered together, it's easier to discuss your estate plan with those who will be impacted.

I recommend the website Death Over Dinner (www. deathoverdinner.org) to my clients looking for tips for having this difficult discussion with family members. The site provides you with ideas about how to talk to your family about topics ranging from your wishes if you are in a coma or vegetative state to how to handle your finances. It even allows you to customize the situation—is it a dinner or a specific holiday, and which family member are you addressing? Is it your parents or a sibling? Death Over Dinner is a great tool for anyone who needs help bringing up this potentially difficult conversation.

You should have these conversations with those directly impacted. Your Uncle Joey in Wisconsin, whom you haven't seen in years, doesn't need to be included, but maybe your aunt who babysits your kids every weekend should be. Any family members who are really involved in your life—whether they be aunts, uncles, or parents—should be in the conversation. If you can gather them all in one room at once to talk, it's like pulling off a Band-Aid—get it done fast, and it hurts less.

The key thing to remember is that legal documents have authority, even over religious preferences. I've seen godparents petition the court to say that, in the eyes of their religion, they are the proper guardians. Unfortunately, without an estate plan, the court still has to approve the custody, and sometimes they don't pick godparents. A grandparent may be given custody over a college friend named as a godparent.

If, for whatever reason, there's only one person requesting custody, they still have to prove that they are capable of taking care of a minor child. This proof must be more than the ability to love the child. They must show their finances, reveal where they live, and say if other kids are living in the home. It's basically an audition before the court.

WHO SHOULD GO TO THE PLANNING MEETINGS?

On occasion I will have parents make an appointment for their adult child to have an estate plan completed, or I'll see a son or daughter come in with their parent for planning. I'm very cautious in these situations because I need to figure out who the client is—is it the child or the parent? I don't want there to be a conflict of interest or an instance of coercion.

If the client is a parent, I'll ask their son or daughter to wait outside, without giving the client an option. This allows me to talk to the parent, and to figure out their mental capacity. Nine out of ten times, this conversation tells me whether the client was coerced to be there. If something feels off, I won't take someone on as a client. This is why it's so important that you don't inhibit yourself in any way when you meet with your lawyer. Stand up for yourself, ask questions, and don't let anyone coerce you into legal decisions.

Once a young woman came in with her mom, at her request. We reached the topic of healthcare, and she was adamant about not being on life support. The mom became frantic and insisted that she would keep her on life support. She appeased her mother and agreed to life support, but after the meeting she called and asked me to change the documents. This is why follow-up calls are important, especially if you're in a meeting where you're feeling controlled by another party. While this may put me in an uncomfortable position, I often encourage young people to attend their planning meeting by themselves, even if they're at the meeting because their parents dragged them there. If the parent is present, I now ask for a solo follow-up to ensure that the needs of my client are being met.

I often meet with clients who are a couple or in a partnership. If they are married and everything is in both their names, I represent both partners and I have them sign a conflict of interest waiver that puts them on notice that they have the right to consult with another attorney at any time. This lets them understand that my duty is to both of them. They will each individually need their own will, but a married couple can have a single trust—or multiple trusts—together.

When everything is in one spouse's name and they plan on creating a trust in only their name, but the other spouse without assets is also present, I make it clear to them that I'm representing the spouse with assets, and the other spouse can speak to a different lawyer for advice. When they are not married, usually both parties will have separate estate planning documents. In this case I usually ask each party to come in alone so the boyfriend or girlfriend doesn't get too assertive in the meeting.

When there are two of you, consider getting a second opinion. Even if the attorney represents both you and your spouse, you should verify that this is not an attorney who has been used by your spouse's family for years. Second opinions ensure that both parties are protected.

This probably all sounds more complicated than you thought, and I know I promised I would make it easy! It's overwhelming now, but it's nothing compared to how overwhelming these elements would be to your family if you didn't take care of them prior to a crisis situation.

If you have questions or concerns on specific situations, don't worry. In the upcoming chapters, you'll find a variety of possible landmines and exactly what to do to avoid them.

PART 2

—

AVOID THE TRAPS

Throughout my time in the legal field, I've seen so many women neglect aspects of their estate planning at various stages of their lives. Here are some of their stories, and how you can avoid their pitfalls. Each chapter will provide you with a key takeaway so that you—or someone you know—can benefit from these lessons.

CHAPTER 4

♥ † ♦

COLLEGE: YOU'RE AN ADULT NOW

Once you turn eighteen, you're an adult in the eyes of the law. Because of this, it's important that you have certain legal documents in order, like an advance healthcare directive and a power of attorney—because unfortunately, anything can happen.

Natalie was a twenty-year-old college student majoring in political science at a school in Northern California. Her divorced parents and two younger siblings still lived in Los Angeles, where she was raised. Natalie had a part-time job and a paid internship with the local city council, and she planned to go to law school. She had been saving her money and finally bought a BMW convertible. Natalie loved her car and felt so independent and free.

Sadly, Natalie was in a major car accident driving home from work one day. She was hit by a drunk driver, and she fell into a coma. Her prognosis was bad. Her iPhone instructed the emergency room to call her parents through its unique emergency feature. Natalie's parents arrived in time for the doctors to say there was no hope for her. Her father said that they needed to pull Natalie off life support; her mother said that their religion did not accept that. Suddenly, there was a war between the parents.

They entered the most emotionally challenging situation of their lives as a divorced couple with resentment and emotional baggage from a long and tumultuous marriage. Now, they faced a major disagreement. Both of them went to court for a conservatorship, a court proceeding in which a judge would determine who would ultimately be allowed to make financial and medical decisions for Natalie. Each parent had to hire their own attorney, and they had to file a petition with the court. In the meantime, Natalie still had bills that needed to be paid—college tuition, rent, utilities, car payment, and credit card expenses. She received financial aid that was directly deposited into her bank account—but there was no financial power of attorney, so Natalie's parents needed to wait until the court gave them access to the bank accounts. This could take a very long time, so Natalie's father paid the bills, since he was in a more secure financial position.

The situation grew even more complicated because Natalie had previously inherited money from her grandmother. The money sat in a bank account that wasn't titled in the name of a trust. Natalie's mother argued that her ex-husband was trying to pull the plug so that he could inherit this large sum of money since, legally, Natalie's parents were next in line to split her bank account.

Natalie's siblings now suffered from grief and lack of attention because their parents were so caught up with Natalie and the courts. They felt as if their parents were ignoring them in favor of the legal proceeding. The money that her parents saved for her two siblings to attend college was now going toward Natalie's legal and medical bills.

In order for this situation to have been avoided, Natalie should have hired a legal professional to prepare an advance healthcare directive and power of attorney for her the minute she turned eighteen. She could have chosen the person who would act on her behalf if she became incapacitated, and she could have decided for herself whether or not she wanted to be on life support. This is such a hard decision for a parent, and a simple legal document removes that burden from them by saying, "Look, if I'm in this situation, I don't want you guys fighting over it, and I don't want to be on life support." Even if Natalie had chosen her mother to be her power of attorney, her mother could not have placed Natalie on life support if she dictated in her advance healthcare directive that she wished not to be on life support. The person you designate as your agent in these documents must follow your wishes. These documents would have ensured no court involvement, no fighting, no legal bills, and no sibling resentment during a catastrophic life event.

Ideally, colleges should partner with law firms to bring legal professionals to their orientation week in the fall. That way, students and parents have the opportunity to hear the importance of having these legal documents in place. Even if a parent pays for insurance and healthcare, once your child turns eighteen you cannot call the hospital and ask questions. This information is confidential, and with no legal document in place that allows you access, your hands are tied.

TAKEAWAYS

Once you turn eighteen, it's time to establish an advance healthcare directive and power of attorney, at a bare minimum. Get these decisions in writing. You don't really know what your parents would do if something happens to you. Take control of your own life, and make your own decisions. Decide whether you want to be an organ donor, and whether you want to be on life support. Think about preferred doctors, burial instructions, and plot locations.

Consider any strong religious beliefs—perhaps you don't want blood transfusions or psychiatric medications administered. It's hard for anyone to fathom not being invincible, especially at eighteen, but things happen.

If you're a parent, this is the last scenario you want to consider, but if you don't, it can ruin the lives of your other kids and family members. Prepare your kids to make these decisions before they go to college.

Once these documents are finalized, the son or daughter holds on to the original and provides a copy for their parents or the person they have selected to make decisions for them. The child can file the healthcare directive with their general doctor or with the school medical center, although this is not necessary—and not my preference, because sometimes the hospital will follow it before the agent even arrives. I've seen instances where a client may have changed their mind on a particular decision and not refiled their healthcare directive with the hospital. Once it's on file, the medical center follows what they have available.

CHAPTER 5

♥ † 💎

YOUR TWENTIES: YOU'RE NOT AS INVINCIBLE AS YOU FEEL

When you're a professional in your midtwenties, the last thing you want to think about is what's going to happen to your money and assets, but now is the time to make a plan. This is especially true if you have a family member who would automatically inherit your assets, and they lack the proper mental or physical capacity to properly manage that money.

At twenty-eight, Lauren was a public relations profes-sional who did very well for herself. She was a homeowner, and she inherited a large sum of money from her deceased parents. Lauren was single with no kids, and she held the common misconception that she didn't need to worry about estate planning—that estate planning was for married couples with children.

During a routine physical, Lauren was shocked to learn that she had stage-four breast cancer.

Lauren had a younger sister named Roxy, who was twenty-four. Roxy was a wild child who had been in and out of rehab several times, and she was terrible with relationships, with a penchant for picking partners who were bad influences. Unfortunately, their parents had always enabled Roxy with money and a desire to take care of her. When they died, she received her inheritance as a restrictionless lump sum, which she blew through rather quickly.

Lauren passed away within the year. At the point when she was diagnosed, she was not in the state of mind to research or plan accordingly for her estate, or for taking care of Roxy. Roxy hired an attorney and inherited Lauren's home, which she immediately sold and liquidated the cash. She also inherited Lauren's share of their parents' inheritance, walking away with $2 million.

Within six months, the money was gone. Roxy spent it on drugs, lavish trips, and dinners with her shady boyfriends.

Just a year after Lauren's death, Roxy found herself penniless. She had no family to lean on, no higher education, and no access to private drug treatments. She was forced onto the street.

Before she passed, Lauren could have gone to an attorney and put all of her assets into a trust. That way, she could have helped Roxy by naming a trustee to manage the money for her, with conditions and restrictions on how Roxy could access that money. Having these documents ultimately would have allowed Lauren to control her money—and how it would be distributed—from the grave. She could have written in rent conditions, monthly spending stipulations, and drug-testing guidelines. The trustee would have been instructed to pay all her expenses directly and never give Roxy the money to do what she wished with it. Lauren even could have forced Roxy to attend a two-year community college so she could begin to earn a solid income and stabilize her life with a degree.

I see this scenario play out time and time again in estate planning. Lives are ruined when people with personal issues inherit huge lump sums and blow right through them.

TAKEAWAYS

Just because you're young and single doesn't mean you

shouldn't have a plan for your assets. You don't want to wait until you have a terminal illness to make this plan. Trust me, with all the chemicals and unhealthy additives in our food, I'm seeing more and more young people neglect their health and die prematurely. Sudden accidents can also take the life of a young person.

It's so important to take control of your life and get these documents in place. You can control your assets, your money, and your real estate from the grave. You can even put long-term conditions in place to take care of your loved ones after you're gone. This is the great thing about estate planning—you actually have a say after your death.

CHAPTER 6

♥ † 💎

COHABITATING: THE PRICE OF LIVING TOGETHER

In today's society, there are many people who decide that they don't necessarily want to get married, but still cohabitate. In this chapter, I discuss two cautionary tales of women who lived with partners and encountered unforeseen hardships, and how a cohabitation agreement could have alleviated some of the stress that comes along with a breakup.

ERICA: EVICTION NOTICE

When I met Erica, she was forty and divorced. She married for the first time when she was young, so she had teen children who decided to live with their father. Erica was a prosperous fashion designer with an immaculately styled home and a great sense of style.

Erica met Don, a financially unstable guy in his early thirties. He had never been married, and he had no kids, but he was in a lot of debt. He wanted to move in with Erica right away, but her mother worried that the relationship was moving too quickly. Don also had a lot of tension with Erica's kids.

Eight months into the relationship, Erica discovered the dark side of Don. He was sloppy, he was lazy, and he drank all the time. Eventually, he was fired from his part-time job. Erica wanted to break up with him, but she learned that she had to legally evict him. Don started getting bills there, changed his address on his driver's license and voter registration, and used the address to file his income tax returns. Her house was now considered his primary residence as well.

After six months, Erica was able to evict him, but she had never thought that she would have to hire an attorney and go through the eviction process for an ex-boyfriend. He wasn't included on the mortgage, but that didn't matter— her home was still his home. During the months it took for the eviction proceedings, she would come home to him on her couch, receiving messages from his new girlfriend. She was paying for utilities, mortgage, food, and so on. It was a complete nightmare.

TARA: HAVING TO START OVER

Tara was an administrative assistant in her early thirties when she met Frank, an established attorney in his late thirties. He wanted his cake and wanted to eat it, too; he was the guy who said that marriage was just a piece of paper, but still liked having Tara as a companion in his life.

Tara wanted to get married and have kids. To relieve the pressure in a sort of *layaway plan*, Frank suggested that Tara move into his house. I see this scenario all the time; guys buy themselves time by asking their marriage-ready girlfriends to move in instead of proposing marriage.

Tara was in complete denial that their relationship was at a dead end. She believed that because she moved in, she was going to marry Don. He denied her friends' hesitance and warnings by saying that this was the biggest commitment he'd ever made to a girlfriend. She should have been grateful, in his eyes.

Don controlled all the bills and the lease, and Tara didn't contribute because the mortgage and utilities were in his name. She spent a good chunk of her salary redecorating the house to turn his bachelor pad into a cozy home for two. He even suggested that she quit her job so she could stay home, which she did. While she took this request as a prelude to marriage, he was really just being selfish and controlling.

After a year, Don broke up with Tara and told her to get out.

Unlike Erica's situation above, Tara didn't force Frank to make her leave, even though his home was technically her primary residence. Tara was so distraught that she simply packed up her things and moved back in with her mom. She had to find a job after a year of being out of the workforce, and she had no return on the money and time she spent remodeling his house and improving his life. At that age, it can be difficult for women to start over—in love and in career. When we take that time off, we lose our connections. Time passes differently for men and women. Society pushes us to believe that men in their late thirties and early forties are more attractive than women in this age range. Don still had time to meet someone and have kids, but Tara had to start all over.

COHABITATION AGREEMENTS

Both Tara and Erica could have protected themselves with a cohabitation agreement. This document, signed by both parties, divides responsibility, decides what constitutes residency and a gift, and determines responsibility for certain bills. It can also state how long someone can stay in the home in the event of a breakup.

Most often, these situations have one person who is the breadwinner or homeowner. The homeowner should have the ability to tell their former partner when they need to leave. One of my clients added a clause to her cohabitation agreement that stated that in the event of their breakup, he had seven days to leave the house. We were clear that this was not his primary residence, and we set up a trust for her so that the house would go to her kids. He couldn't go to court and try to stake a claim in her property.

Another one of my clients bought a home with her partner because of loan purposes; she was doing a lot of freelance work, and she didn't qualify for a loan on her own. She paid for the entire down payment through an inheritance. I warned her that it was very important that we state in her agreement that she paid for the down payment. He was only on the title for loan purposes. We calculated the responsibilities of each party for mortgage payments and improvement costs in the event of a breakup, and we even wrote provisions for inflation in the agreement, depending on the length of their relationship.

I've found that with these cohabitation agreements, it's

rarely the couple who comes to me requesting the documentation. Friends or family members push them toward it for protection. Couples fall in love, and they don't think about this kind of thing when they're on cloud nine. They normally are so happy that they've found a partner whom they want to live with, and they don't want to bother with gruesome details. Unfortunately, nasty breakups are a reality, and the last thing anyone wants is to have their ex living in their home indefinitely.

In my experience, people appear to be marrying less frequently nowadays, and cohabitation agreements are becoming more common, although most people are still unaware that they even exist. Only about 10 percent of my clients have had one drafted; however, cohabitation agreements are replacing prenups, in a way. Couples drafting cohabitation agreements often have had prior marriages and are worried about the aftermath of a breakup.

Sometimes, one party is so offended by the request that the relationship stalls out and they either don't move in or they break up altogether. Other couples, however, are completely comfortable with the situation and simply want to live together with nothing from the other person.

TAKEAWAYS

When you are cohabitating, you need to make sure that you have a clear understanding of each other's expectations, and of what will happen if the relationship ends. Living together puts you at a higher risk than you think. It's not like college where you're just hanging out with your boyfriend. Your partner is not just a roommate. Roommates usually share a lease, and there is an agreement that splits the payment or dictates that one party is paying the other a certain amount for living there with particular conditions for sharing a residence.

Don't assume that your partner sees living together as a prelude to marriage. Be clear about your expectations, about expenses, and about the results of a breakup. Just like with a prenuptial agreement, cohabitation agreements really can preserve the romance because they establish clarity in the relationship.

CHAPTER 7

♥ † ◆

MARRIAGE AND DIVORCE: TALKING PRENUPTIAL AGREEMENTS

A prenuptial agreement (also referred to as a prenup) is a legal agreement that determines what will happen to your own and your spouse's assets and income in the event of a divorce, separation, or death.

California is currently one of ten community property states—the others being Arizona, Idaho, Louisiana, Nevada, New Mexico, Texas, Washington, and Wisconsin. Alaska allows for opt-in community property. Community property states that any property or income acquired during the marriage (except for gifts or inheritance) will be divided equally by both spouses in a divorce or death. A prenup allows for agreed changes to this division. These agreements still have a stigma in the world of marrying couples, but unfortunately, in the aftermath of a possible divorce, life will be difficult if you find yourself without one.

Below are three common scenarios.

LILY AND TODD: HIDING INCOME

Lily was a young woman in her early twenties when she started dating Todd, a wealthy real estate heir also in his early twenties. His family owned the real estate company they both worked for. Todd was infatuated with Lily, and she agreed to stop working at his suggestion, as often happens in these cases. He traveled all the time for work. They got engaged, and she planned on having kids right after they got married.

Lily signed a prenup that she didn't bother to read and hired an attorney referred by Todd's attorney who did a poor job in explaining the agreement; she was just so excited about marrying someone like Todd. After eight years of marriage, Lily was still home with their three daughters. Unfortunately, they decided to divorce. When Lily referenced back to the prenup, she realized that she was entitled to very little spousal support. It stipulated that she got a percentage of his income, but Todd had been sneaky; he was worth a lot, but his family only allocated him a small percentage on payroll to help him disguise his income.

Since they were divorcing below the ten-year mark, Lily wouldn't get a dime over the amount stipulated in the prenup, which said that if they were married less than ten years, she would get less in spousal support. California is one of the few states where, if you earn less than your spouse and have been married for at least ten years, there's a tendency to get spousal support for as long as you need it, from the spouse that makes more money than you. Usually this spousal support is paid until the receiving spouse gets remarried.

Unfortunately, Lily had no access to that. In addition, the money that was set aside for their daughters was held in a trust for when they were older, so Lily would have no access to those funds either.

Her lifestyle was severely downgraded.

With three young kids, Lily had to get back into real estate. She had been out of the workforce for a decade, so she had no contacts. If Lily had been more careful in reading and reviewing the prenup, she could have stipulated a lot of different elements that I will discuss below.

ERIN AND BEN: NEGOTIATING THE PRENUP

Erin was in a similar scenario to Lily. She was head over heels in love with Ben, and she didn't want to work. Her future in-laws were fine with her not working, and they contacted their family lawyer to work on a prenup for Erin and their son.

Erin's friends told her that she should hire her own attorney to protect herself, despite the help from her in-laws. She hired me as her personal lawyer, and I read the agreement. I found several negotiation points that could be used to her advantage. Instead of getting a small percentage of Ben's income, I negotiated a more comfortable amount. And, believe it or not, I removed a clause that stated that she would be paid more if she gave birth to a son rather than a daughter (I see these bizarre provisions in prenups all the time).

There was also a clause in Erin's original prenup that stated that any gifts over a certain amount should not be considered a gift, and they would need to be returned in the event of a divorce. So, if her husband bought her an expensive car, a piece of jewelry, or a fur coat, she would need to return that if they divorced. I removed this clause as well.

Because I was basing her spousal support on her fiancé's income, I needed to know his income trends so I could negotiate up. I asked for the last three to five years of his tax returns to determine these trends.

Ben's attorney was completely thrown off by my pushback. There were many heated arguments between us, and he told me that in the twenty years he had drafted prenups, he had never seen this much pushback. My response was that it was time for him to change the standard clauses he had been using, and it was time for him and for his clients to advance with society. In the end, the prenup was changed to Erin's advantage.

In California and in several other states, good attorneys insist that the couple hire two separate attorneys to represent them in drafting the prenup, since it's a conflict of interest to represent both parties. If you are going to limit spousal support, there's also a required seven-day window that requires the document to be presented at least seven days in advance of signing. This way, you cannot hand a prenup to your partner the day before your wedding. If one party waives spousal support or alimony, by law, they must have two attorneys—one who will draft the agreement, and another who will review it for the second party.

It is common, as was the case of Lily and Todd, that the wealthier partner pays for the legal fees of their fiancé. Another common trend is selecting an attorney whom the drafting attorney recommends. Don't fall for this—pick your attorney so that you ensure that you're comfortable with them.

MARY AND BRIAN: PRESERVING THE ROMANCE

Mary was an ob-gyn in her midthirties with her own practice when she met Brian online. He was an attractive musician, also in his midthirties. Online dating was the fastest and most convenient way for Mary to meet someone, but it didn't allow her to thoroughly investigate him. Mary's parents were very unhappy that Brian didn't have a professional status, because that was important to them. They preferred Mary to be with another doctor, lawyer, or businessman.

Mary, on the other hand, loved that Brian was different from anyone she had ever dated. He actually listened to her, and he was not intimidated by her or her success. Brian had a lot of student loans and credit card debt, and Mary's parents worried about them getting serious in their relationship. Mary was a strong woman, though, with her own business. She didn't feel like she needed to listen to her parents, so she moved forward. They got engaged.

Mary's parents pushed for a prenup, but Mary thought she was choosing love and trust over making Brian sign an agreement. The two were married for five years and they had a young son when they ended up divorcing. The excitement Mary had in the beginning of their relationship, when she was marrying a hot, badass musician, was gone. During the divorce proceedings, the court looked at various factors—including Mary's income and travel schedule, and that she took care of the bills while Brian took care of the home front. She had created a standard of living for them, and the court awarded Brian full custody of their son, and she had to pay child and spousal support.

To add insult to injury, Brian got a percentage of her business because it grew during their time together. In California, if an asset increases in value during your marriage, your spouse is entitled to half of the increased value. He tapped into her retirement accounts, too, since she started putting money away once they were married and had their son. Mary had enabled Brian by paying off the debt he acquired before their marriage. She had made everything so easy for him, and she created patterns. Now, she had to continue paying the debt he acquired during their marriage, too.

Mary could have completely protected herself by having a prenup in place. She could have stipulated that the income generated from her business was her separate property. Not only was she entitled to do this, but she should have; after all, it was a business she created before marriage, and she was the working spouse. But, in the eyes of the law, Brian was entitled to the profits because his job was staying home and taking care of the family. The courts could have claimed that the business thrived because Mary had more time at the office when Brian was taking care of the household.

At the very least, Mary could have stated in a prenup that Brian's existing debt and his debt during marriage were his, and that she was not responsible for paying it. The new acquisitions could have been split evenly.

The only thing that cannot be discussed in a prenup is child support and child custody. Sometimes in these cases, one spouse will try to get full custody of the child, not necessarily because they want to care for them full-time, but because they want the child support. Not only did Brian get alimony, but he also received child support because he was granted full custody. He was technically in complete control of the child support and of how he decided to use it. Mary had no way of ensuring that Brian actually used the money for their son.

TAKEAWAYS

I look at prenups like an insurance policy. So many marriages end in divorce. And today, women are more confident about protecting themselves. Women are marrying later in life because they're going to school and focusing on their careers, and they don't feel the pressure to marry early like previous generations. With this change of attitude comes the security and independence of being able to stand on their own two feet, and we need to protect that. It's not just the money they've earned or the success that they have; a lot of women come from very successful families and have substantial inheritances. They need to protect the wealth that their families worked hard to earn. Thus, your takeaway for this chapter is to get a prenup before getting married!

Remember, a prenup covers more than just money and large assets—it can also stipulate debt and intellectual property, include cheating clauses, and so on. If your fiancé is prone to cheating and there's a lot of money at stake, a cheating clause will provide the additional protection you may want in your marriage. No one is here to judge what you want in your marriage, or in your agreement. This is a document to protect you.

If you get married and don't have a prenup, explore a postnuptial agreement (postnup). In the example above, when Mary started noticing some red flags during the time they were married, she could have created a postnup. This is recommended for couples who start out with only a few assets or maybe nothing at all, and their situation then changes dramatically. Maybe one of the spouses becomes successful in their field, starts a company, or writes a book. Postnups are more difficult once you're married, because you cannot force your spouse to sign the agreement. You are already married, and it's much harder to walk away from the marriage. If they're entitled to more than what the postnup stipulates, it would be to their disadvantage to sign. However, it is an option you can explore.

Some couples also put a sunset clause in their agreement. After a certain number of years, the prenup expires, and they go back to the drawing board to renegotiate the terms. I know some attorneys are not fans of the sunset clause, but I like it because it's a great tool that allows couples to revisit their original document down the road, after situations may have changed.

Really, a prenup can include clauses for nearly any concern. I've seen everything from "porky clauses," if a spouse gains a certain amount of weight, to cheating clauses. The possibilities are endless.

DISCUSSING THE TOPIC WITH YOUR FIANCÉ

Many people worry about bringing up the topic of a prenup. For me personally, when I'm dating someone, I bring up the idea of prenups in conversation to gauge where the other person stands on the subject. Perhaps there is a celebrity case in the news, or a friend who's drafting their own, but I find a way to transition to the subject without offending the person I'm dating.

In my opinion, prenups actually preserve the romance. When you're on good terms with your future spouse, why not take the opportunity to discuss what would happen if you decide to separate? If you can't talk about a prenup when you're infatuated and in love, imagine trying to talk about dividing assets when you despise the person and want a divorce. Prenups are there to serve and protect us, so they really shouldn't be viewed negatively.

Of course, that doesn't mean the discussion is always a success. There are times I've drafted agreements and the engagement falls through because of it. While the client may be upset at the time, I tell them that if their partner wasn't willing to sign the document, they should take it as a sign that the person wasn't a good match. Prenups are great tools to see if the other person really loves you for you, or if they're simply concerned about money or getting something in return from the union.

You need to be concerned about yourself, your family, and your children, and a prenup helps you do exactly that.

CHAPTER 8

♥ † ♦

KIDS: PREPARE FOR THE UNTHINKABLE

In this chapter, we discuss what happens to your children in the event that you're no longer around. This may be a tough topic, because no one wants to think of that day coming.

Diane was a stay-at-home mom in her early forties married to a successful doctor named Linda. They had two daughters, ages two and five, and they figured that if something happened to them, Diane's sister, Isabelle, would step in. Isabelle was a single banker, and she lived five minutes away from their residence. She had been in the girls' lives since they were born.

One day, Diane and Linda were driving with their daughters when they were hit, head-on, by another car. The girls were okay, but both women died from their injuries. Isabelle was in complete shock and grief over losing her sister and her sister-in-law, and she went into protection mode. She took the girls and called an attorney.

As I discussed before, so often people think that it will be easy for their parents, siblings, or the people they name godparents to step in and take custody, but this was not the case, as neither Diane nor Linda had a will that stated guardianship.

Isabelle went before the court to take custody of her nieces and said that she knew their parents wanted her to raise them. The judge needed her to prove that she was in a position to care for the girls and raise them, in both income and living conditions. They wanted to see that the girls would have the best care possible.

Because she didn't have a lot of money in the bank, Isabelle began gathering information and liquidating some of her retirement accounts and investments to show that she could financially support her nieces. Meanwhile, Linda's sister, Kate, flew in from Wisconsin to claim the kids. Kate was socially conservative, and she rarely saw them, having estranged herself from Linda because of Linda's lifestyle choices. Kate was married, wealthy, stayed home, and had already raised her own kids.

Kate was awarded custody because she was seen as more fit in the eyes of the court. Despite Isabelle's taking all the steps necessary to prove her financial stability, and despite being close to the kids their entire lives, she became the aunt who lived many states away and only got to see her nieces on holidays.

The minute they had kids, Diane and Linda should have visited an attorney and prepared a will. In their will, they could have decided the guardians of their minor children. People don't like to think about not being there for their kids, but this is such an important step in protecting them.

PREPARING A WILL

If you have a partner, I suggest that as you prepare your will, you make a ranked list of the five people you want to have custody of your children. Compare the two lists and see where they overlap. If the kids are designated to a couple, one person should be listed as the primary guardian in case that couple gets a divorce.

Be extremely detailed about how you want your kids raised. When you make this decision, it's important to consider a variety of elements. Who lives close, who wants the responsibility of raising children, and most important, who has beliefs that line up with your own? Who has the same religious beliefs? Who has the same political beliefs? Who would provide the kids the same medical care and diet that you do? These may sound like minute details, but these are all aspects of raising a child. Think of Diane and Linda. The children lived in a progressive family and were closer to their Aunt Isabelle, who is more liberally minded, than their Aunt Kate. Kate is very conservative, and didn't even agree with Linda's lifestyle choices to begin with. Now, the kids are placed in a family that doesn't align with the beliefs of the home where they were raised their entire lives.

Even when you select a guardian and your decision is documented, the courts still have to approve your selection. It's best to select someone who will easily be approved, and this requires considering geography. If you choose a guardian who lives in New York and you live in California, if something happens to you and your child is a junior in high school, the courts will consider a variety of factors. Courts aren't likely to impose that a minor move high schools and across the country when the child is nearly an adult or has two months left to graduate. If your third cousin who lives down the street comes to the court, the court may have preference for that person even though your will specified someone in New York.

FUNDING YOUR CHILD'S CARE

If you give the responsibility of guardianship to someone,

you want to make sure that there is money available for them to raise your kids. No matter their financial status, this responsibility adds a burden to the people you select, especially if they have children of their own. Your assets should be designated toward a trust for your children, and you may or may not have the same people managing the trust that you have raising them. You may have one guardian for your children's financial needs, and one guardian to physically take care of them, decide where they live, and choose which schools they will attend. Having two guardians is beneficial if you have someone in your life who is really good at managing money, but another who is warmhearted as a parent and knows how to care for a child. If you go on this path, it's best that these guardians get along and are on the same page.

In a trust, you can also designate when your kids will inherit their money with special clauses. Maybe they need to be a certain age, or perhaps they are not allowed to smoke. I've even seen some parents add a clause that states that if their child goes to UCLA, they receive less money from the trust because they are a diehard Trojan from UCLA's big rival, USC.

Educational restrictions are often included in trust clauses, stating that a child must get a bachelor's degree or some other form of education to have access to the money. I don't like adding these educational requirements, because when trusts are first documented, children are often young. Parents don't know if their child may become diagnosed with a learning disorder; or maybe, school is simply not for them. I've seen very successful children make millions with only a high school diploma because they're so savvy and business oriented. I do, however, encourage employment restrictions, such as proof of a job for a certain amount of time, or mandatory drug testing if the child has problems with substance abuse.

I also encourage parents to think about not giving their children money in a lump sum. Allocating the trust money into two or three stages encourages more responsibility. Maybe they receive 50 percent at age twenty-five, and 50 percent at thirty. After all, you don't know how your children will manage money down the road. You can also allocate different restrictions for each child. Maybe you have a sixteen-year-old who's smarter with money than your twenty-one-year-old, and you want the younger child to get their full allotment at eighteen, before their older sibling.

Some parents require that their child obtain a prenup if they decide to get married. This stipulation must be met before they get their inheritance. Not only does this allow parents to protect their children from the grave, but it also gives their kids a way to blame the prenup requirement on their parents.

These decisions are up to you when you create a trust, but these are all elements to consider, and the great thing about trusts is that you can change them. Most of them are revocable, meaning that they can be updated. As your children grow and change, you can change the trust stipulations. I always advise clients to revisit the documents when major life changes happen—for example, a death, birth, new property, loss of a job, new income, and so on. Any changes made to the trust stipulations are charged at an hourly fee.

TAKEAWAYS

Create a will as soon as your children are born. This especially holds true for single women. Perhaps you have full custody of your child because the biological father is unable to be a good parent and hasn't been involved in your child's life. If so, get your wishes in writing. In situations like this, the court almost always automatically gives full custody of a child to the other parent when one dies. So if there's a reason that you feel that the other parent should not take care of your child, write your will as soon as you can.

Make sure that you talk to the designees beforehand. This is a huge responsibility, and you don't want to surprise them with a letter announcing that they're now parents after you're gone.

Don't assume that someone important in your child's life will automatically be approved to take care of your kids. Make sure that the person you select is financially established, and that they have a home big enough to raise kids.

Reevaluate the conditions of the trust you create as time goes by, and update these conditions as you get to know your child and their needs.

Finally, make sure that the guardian and trustee you select can work together as a team, for the benefit of your child.

CHAPTER 9

♥ † 💎

STARTING OVER: REMARRIAGE AND BLENDING YOUR FAMILY

This chapter will show you the importance of anticipating conflicts with children and existing assets when blending families together. Here are two stories of two sets of remarrying clients.

SHARON AND JACK: NEGATING INTENTIONS

Sharon was in her early fifties and owned a tech company. She had a significant amount of assets with investments and real estate in Southern California.

After eighteen months of dating, Sharon decided to marry Jack, a high school science teacher in his midfifties. With his permission, she added Jack as a trustee in her existing trust and designated him as the primary beneficiary with the assumption that he would follow her wishes. Outside of the trust paperwork, Sharon discussed with Jack that each of her children would inherit a house upon her death; Bobby, twenty-four, would get the Palm Springs home, and Jennifer, twenty-six, would get the house in Newport Beach.

Both children knew of their mother's intent, as Jennifer loved the Newport Beach home and Bobby always had a great time at the Palm Springs home. They also both knew of their mother's other focuses—she supported a specific charity, and her sister needed money because she wasn't doing well financially. Sharon also owned a home in Laguna Beach where the kids vacationed as a family. All the art and furniture inside that home was meaningful to them.

Sadly, Sharon passed away, and Jack went rogue. He arranged a funeral that didn't reflect her wishes and immediately liquidated all her assets. He changed the locks on all the houses, and within only a couple of months, he moved his new girlfriend into the house he shared with Sharon. Sharon's children were left with nothing.

The problem was that once Sharon married Jack and added him as a trustee and beneficiary of her trust, her undocumented intentions went out the window. Her children could have litigated the trust, but it would have taken a long time, and it would have been difficult to prove that their mom didn't want Jack in control of her estate. The court always goes with documents as points of reference for the person's intentions. Sharon had, after all, added Jack to the trust and didn't stipulate her children's inheritances. Lawyers couldn't know what Jack and Sharon discussed outside their meetings, and the court couldn't know her intent unless she created the proper documentation.

So, what should have Sharon done? She should have kept the same trust she had before she married Jack, and she never should have added him. She could have updated it with specific instructions for him as a way of comingling her life with his once they married, but this is not my recommendation. People often do this to prove to their new spouse that "what's mine is ours," but when you have children from previous relationships, most of your big assets should remain with them. Sharon could have designated that a flat rate or certain accounts would go to Jack so that he felt secure and protected, but this is as far as she should have taken it.

JOHANNA AND ANNETTE: ANGRY CHILDREN

Johanna, an art dealer, and Annette, an accountant, met in their midforties and began dating. Both had children from prior marriages, and they had modest assets when they became a couple, choosing to rent a home in the beginning.

They began to do well financially in their respective careers, purchased a vacation home in Santa Barbara, and added valuable art as they remodeled. They put all the children—Johanna's adopted son from her prior marriage, and Annette's biological kids—on one trust.

Johanna died after a long battle with ovarian cancer; four years later, Annette died of a heart attack. They had set up their trust so each child received an equal share, and any decisions must be made by a majority of the trustees. Since there were three kids, two out of the three could agree on something and take action, even if the third disagreed. Annette's children were still angry that their mother left their father to be with Johanna. They decided to liquidate all the assets, and Johanna's son, with only one-third of the vote, had no power to override them. He also found it unfair that they each got a one-third share, since half of the assets were his mom's—he should have had half, too. He knew that there was a significant value in the art his mother acquired before she married Annette. Still, there was no stipulation in the trust about the art and whom it should go to.

Considering their family history and tension, what should have Johanna and Annette done to protect all their kids? They should have designated an independent person, whether an attorney, an adviser, or a friend, to make these decisions. They should have divided assets by the two sides of the family rather than by the number of kids. Also, decisions could have been stipulated as unanimous; if they could not be, a fourth person could have been used as a tiebreaker vote. This process would have ensured fair distribution. Although they tried to make everything fair, they didn't account for the resentment from Annette's kids.

TAKEAWAYS

When you remarry, make sure your children are protected. Your intentions should be clear through written instructions. The court isn't privy to your late-night conversations with your partner, so document all decisions. And if you're no longer around and your spouse remarries, no one can touch certain assets you've designated for your kids.

Anytime you experience a major life change, reexamine your documents and update them. And make sure everyone, including your children, is on the same page. Everyone thinks that kids cannot handle these big conversations, but they can. Imagine not having these conversations, then all of a sudden receiving a legal document stating how your life is going to be after your parent's passing. You need to talk to your children about your mindset. If you know there is tension, designate an unbiased person to help mediate and make decisions.

CHAPTER 10

♥ † 💎

TAKE BACK THE REINS: WHAT TO DO WHEN EVERYTHING CHANGES

Life often throws a curveball at you. It's important to have your estate plan in place, but it's equally important to know the current state of your finances, especially if your partner usually manages them.

In this chapter, I'll share a story about a woman in her early sixties whose husband left her, forcing her to confront the state of her assets for the first time in her life. I'll also discuss a woman whose devoted husband kept her in the dark about his business dealings, leaving her in a precarious position when he died unexpectedly.

HOLLY AND RICHARD: A HUMILIATING DIVORCE

Holly was in her midsixties and married to Richard, a partner at a successful law firm. She was a stay-at-home mom for thirty-five years and was now very active with her grandkids and within her church and community.

While Richard built his career, Holly entertained and took care of the kids. One day she received a fraud alert and went online to review their credit card statement. She found expensive online purchases and confronted Richard. He came clean and admitted to buying gifts for Katherine, another lawyer at his firm—they had been having a long-term affair.

Holly gave Richard an ultimatum and told him to stop the affair immediately; Richard refused. After more than thirty-five years of marriage, Holly was served with divorce papers in public. She was shocked and humiliated.

She hired an attorney and found that she would not get as much spousal support as she originally thought, since Richard had been hiding money under names of family members. He had been anticipating the day he would divorce Holly, and because she wasn't on top of the finances, she had been unaware of what he was doing.

Holly failed to find an aggressive attorney or hire a forensic accountant to find a paper trail for Richard's money.

She was forced to move in with her elderly mother until she could get back on her feet.

What should Holly have done differently? She should have made a retirement account, and she should have set money aside. She didn't have Social Security income, because she was a stay-at-home mom and she wasn't technically in the workforce. Her accountant should have been separate from Richard's, and she should have had her own financial adviser or lawyer. They could have walked her through worst-case scenarios if something went wrong.

Also, Holly should have been more involved in how the couple reported their taxes. If things didn't add up, she could have asked questions. Since Richard's payroll was so low, where was his cash coming from? She could have insisted on paper statements, so nothing could be hidden in online banking.

Sometimes women can have an old-school mentality that their husband takes care of all the finances and deals with the accountants and lawyers. Unfortunately, this can go wrong. Holly never thought that Richard would leave her for a twenty-eight-year-old. He was a devoted father, and she thought he was a devoted husband. There was no way he would ever plan on leaving her after all those years. Richard used Holly, and Holly should have protected herself and educated herself about the finances, not only because he had the potential to cheat and leave her, but he could have passed away and she would have no clue what to do—like in the next example.

LISA AND AMAN: FAILURE TO PREPARE

Lisa was in her early thirties when she married Aman, a gentleman in his fifties with one child from a previous relationship.

After several years of marriage, Aman had a heart attack that he did not survive. Lisa discovered that their family home and the commercial properties he managed were in his name only. Normally one name is used for loan purposes when one spouse has better credit than the other. Because the title of their house was just in his name, Lisa had to go through a probate process to secure the home. She tried to call the lender to gather information about payments, but the lender wouldn't speak to her, because she was not on the title.

Lisa had a little cash from bank accounts, but it wouldn't get her through the probate process. The filing fee for probate was roughly $500, and she needed to hire an attorney, who would charge anywhere from $2,500 to $5,000 for a retainer agreement. Lisa borrowed money from friends and family to get through probate; all the while she had to deal with tenants from the commercial property, a task she had never handled previously.

Her attorney was shady and took advantage of her. Her tenants took advantage of her, too. Lisa was on a sinking ship.

Aman wasn't trying to screw her over; he just didn't think ahead. He never could have predicted the heart attack, but he should have put everything in a trust, so even though he was the only one on the loan, he could have named who would succeed him and own the property if something happened to him. He should have made sure that Lisa knew where all the legal paperwork for the assets were, such as the deeds for the commercial property. Lisa should have known who the tenants were, the history of the building, and about any lease agreements. Even if she wasn't involved in the daily operations, she should have known who all the major players were, like the lawyers, operation manager, and repairman.

Since the title was only in the husband's name, Lisa only received her one-third share of the real estate. The remaining two-thirds went to his child. This was infuriating since Lisa had financially contributed to this real estate as well.

TAKEAWAYS

You're probably reading this and wondering why women tend to neglect their financial lives throughout marriage. I think that women are so good at multitasking, they get caught up in taking care of their kids without taking care of themselves. They put themselves last. This is where we can change: it's time to start making ourselves a priority. This isn't being selfish; it's being protective—protective of ourselves, and protective of our children, if we have them. If we don't start taking care of ourselves, we won't be able to take care of our loved ones.

You must put yourself and your finances first. Take the story of Teresa Giudice from *The Real Housewives of New Jersey*. Her husband, Joe, took care of everything, including hiring accountants and applying for loans to purchase real estate. Teresa trusted her husband and would just sign off on the legal documents without reviewing them. They were both convicted of conspiracy to commit mail fraud, wire fraud, and bank fraud, as well as making false statements on loan applications, and had to file for bankruptcy. She ultimately went to jail for something her husband did. Anything can change, no matter how old you are or how set you think you are in life. We aren't always in control.

We can, however, protect our future by insisting on being involved in the daily financial operations of our families.

This might mean having a separate accountant, lawyer, or financial adviser. Have plenty of money set aside for old age, since women live longer than men. As we take care of everyone else, in the end, there's no one left to take care of us—having enough money to live comfortably in old age makes a difference.

CONCLUSION

Let's look again at our four major components of an estate plan:

- An advance healthcare directive for medical decisions
- A durable power of attorney for financial decisions if you become incapacitated
- A will to transfer personal items like jewelry, clothes, and furniture, as well as name a guardian for any minor children
- A trust that will distribute large assets like real estate, businesses, and bank accounts to beneficiaries

If you don't get these things in order, you cause a lot of anxiety for both you and your loved ones if anything should happen to you. Things can turn into financial and emotional disasters in the event of a crisis, because the court will manage and control everything in your life if you don't have these documents in order.

Once these documents are written and signed, you'll have peace of mind. You can rest at night knowing that you've taken that extra step in protecting yourself and your family. The process helps you sort through relationships and goals, and it allows you to see the people who play an important role in your life. You figure out who you can trust and who you can't, and you learn how to be more assertive and organized. You know where your legal documents are, and you have a plan in place for the day you're no longer around. Although the whole process can seem sad and morbid, you're doing a huge service for the people you leave behind.

It's important to have a timeframe for yourself, and to set goals. Give yourself a six-month window when you have time to sit down and plan, like during a vacation or summer holiday. Start by asking around for attorney recommendations; you have nothing to lose in the process and everything to gain. Going through courts is expensive and time consuming. Look at estate planning like any other necessary task in life, like health insurance. This may not be a fun or pleasant discussion, but it's important.

You owe it to yourself, and you owe it to your loved ones.

Feel free to contact me via my website, http://www.baroutilaw.com/.

ACKNOWLEDGMENTS

To my makers, my dear parents Azita and Tony, thank you for always supporting me and sacrificing so much to give me a better life. I am nothing without the both of you.

To my sister, Tina, your creative genius and ability to unapologetically be yourself has inspired me more than you will ever know. I love you.

To my aunt Maryam, my uncle Reza, and my grandparents Jalal and Azar, I am truly blessed to have you all in my life. Thank you for always being by my side.

To my law school professor Kim Dayton, thank you for sparking my interest in estate planning and showing me that the true test of success is how much we can help others.

To my tribe and army of strong women, I would be lost without you: Kerri Kasem for always pushing me to go 10x, Hana Khzam for unconditionally loving me, Darya Lucas for teaching me how to be resilient, Judith Branconier for always believing in my "Oprah" potential, and Krystine Cisto for being the most loving and honest mentor a woman could ever have.

Thank you to my publicists, Rick Krusky and Marlan Willardson, for always taking me to the next level.

To everyone on the Scribe Media team: Ellie Cole, Nikki Katz, Zoe Norvell, Aleks Mendel, Zach Obront, Jesse Sussman, Josh Frank, Ian Claudius, Cristina Ricci, Janina Lawrence, Ash Van Otterloo, and Shannon Lee, thank you for helping me create a piece of work that I am truly proud of.

To everyone at First Broker Realty, I am grateful for each and every one of you. Thank you for always supporting my professional endeavors. A special thanks to Gerry Najarro, a remarkable leader who has inspired so many with his authenticity and courage.

ABOUT THE
AUTHOR

NAZ BAROUTI is a lawyer, author, entrepreneur, media commentator, and public speaker who is well-known in the legal world as an estate planning "guru" and an advocate for women. In 2011, she established Barouti Law Corporation, which now boasts five offices in Southern California. Naz has been featured on Fox News Radio and Bloomberg TV, in *USA Today*, and in other news outlets, providing legal commentary on matters of the death, divorce, and the criminal prosecution of high-profile figures. She cohosted the weekly radio program *Protecting Your Family* with Kerri Kasem and is a board member for the Kasem Cares Foundation.